FOUR STAR
SIGHT READING AND EAR TESTS

Book 8

DAILY EXERCISES FOR PIANO STUDENTS

BY BORIS BERLIN

Revised Edition

Recommended for use in conjunction with the piano examinations of the
Royal Conservatory of Music

ISBN 0-88797-217-9

Printed in Canada

PREFACE

To be able to read at sight is of the first importance to every piano student. And yet so many of them seem to have trouble, with the result that they do not make the progress they should and often lose much of the real joy of being able to play the piano.

Why do they have trouble ?

The main reason is that so very few of them practise reading at sight in any regular and systematic manner. They have an idea—a completely false idea—that reading at sight is a special gift peculiar to rarely endowed students.

Good sight reading is not difficult for any student. It is simply the result of careful preparation and regular use, through daily practice, of the powers of concentration and observation.

Of course there are some students who can read at sight better than others, or who learn to read at sight more quickly and more accurately than others. But these students, too, need regular practice if they want to develop and improve an ability without which no one can acquire true musicianship.

BOOK 8

FOUR STAR
SIGHT READING AND EAR TESTS

DAILY EXERCISES FOR PIANO STUDENTS

BY BORIS BERLIN

FREDERICK
HARRIS
MUSIC

INTRODUCTION

While good sight reading is obviously essential to a would-be professional musician, it is no less important to the amateur. Indeed it stands to reason that, when a student has given up the idea of a musical career (if he ever entertained it), his maintaining or dropping an interest in music as a hobby will depend in almost exact proportion on his ability to read at sight. If he has nothing to play but the few pieces he has learned in his days of music study and no time to practise new ones his interest will soon pall, whereas the good sight reader may keep his interest alive with almost unlimited new material, even though he never brings his playing to a stage of technical excellence fit for public performance. I would therefore remind teachers that sight reading is *not* a "side-line" for any music student: far better let him postpone an examination or two and concentrate. He will easily make up for lost time later.

It should be impressed on a pupil that a mistake once made in sight reading *is* a mistake once and for all, and too late to recall. Having prepared himself as thoroughly as possible a candidate should play steadily — not because he will deceive the examiner if he makes mistakes — but because, for practical purposes the only sight reader worthwhile is the one that keeps going. A wrong note or chord will, to be sure, count against him, but it will doubly count against him if in going back to locate or correct it he makes a break in the rhythm. If he *does* correct it, it is in any case not playing at first sight, but at second. Of course he will keep going satisfactorily only if he has learned to read a beat or more ahead of what he is playing.

SIR ERNEST MacMILLAN
—*"On the Preparation of Ear Tests"*

AIM

The AIM of this series of Graded Books is to help students acquire a fluency in sight reading, and to prepare them for the SIGHT READING and the EAR TEST part of piano examinations.

DESCRIPTION

This book contains eight sets of DAILY SIGHT READING and EAR TEST EXERCISES. Each set should be practised by the student at home in preparation for the FOUR STAR TEST, which will be given by the teacher at the music lesson.

After the last FOUR STAR TEST, the FINAL TEST is given to the student before the issue of the CERTIFICATE OF MERIT.

The student should follow the directions when practising the DAILY SIGHT READING.

Excerpts by the following composers have been used in this book:

J. André (1775-1842)

W.F. Bach (1710-1784)

L. Beethoven (1770-1827)

W. Byrd (1542-1623)

J.B. Duvernoy (1802-1880)

Eiges

A. Eshpay (1925-   )

C.W. Gluck (1714-1787)

G. Grünewald (1675-1739)

J. Hässler (1747-1822)

F.J. Haydn (1732-1809)

J.N. Hummel (1778-1837)

D. Kabalevsky (1904-   )

R. Kellegrew (16th c.)

J.P. Kirnberger (1721-1783)

J.H. Knecht (1752-1817)

F. Kuhlau (1786-1832)

K.M. Kunz (1812-1875)

F. Liszt (1811-1886)

J.B. Lully (1632-1687)

W.A. Mozart (1756-1791)

H. Pachulski (1859-1921)

H. Purcell (1659-1695)

V. Rebikov (1866-1920)

F. Schubert (1797-1828)

L. Spohr (1784-1859)

D. Steibelt (1765-1823)

P.I. Tchaikovsky (1840-1893)

G.P. Telemann (1681-1767)

C. Vogel (1808-1892)

D. Zipoli (1688-1726)

DAILY SIGHT READING FOR TEST No. 1

① DATE ....

This piece is in ____ time. It is in the key of _____ and has ____ sharps/flats.
Play, counting the beats.

Allegretto

LULLY

Before Playing look at the **Clefs, Key-Signature, Time-Signature** and **Fingering**

② DATE ....

Put an X under each appearance of the rhythmic pattern ♩♩♩, then play, naming the left-hand notes.
Play again, naming the right-hand notes.

Allegro non troppo

KUNZ

Clap or tap the rhythm of the melody.

PLAY ONE SET EVERY DAY

③ DATE......................

Mark all the tonic chords (I) with an X.

Play this hymn tune harmonization while singing any voice (part).

KNECHT

Before Playing look at the **Clefs, Key-Signature, Time-Signature** and **Fingering**

④ DATE......................

The tempo of this piece is ___Moderato___ , which means _Not too fast + Not Too slow._

Trace the slurs and phrase marks and copy all the expression marks.

Play with correct expression.

Moderato SCHUBERT

The expression marks found in this piece are: _____

DAILY SIGHT READING FOR TEST No. 1

⑤ Clap or tap the rhythm of the melody.

DATE ....

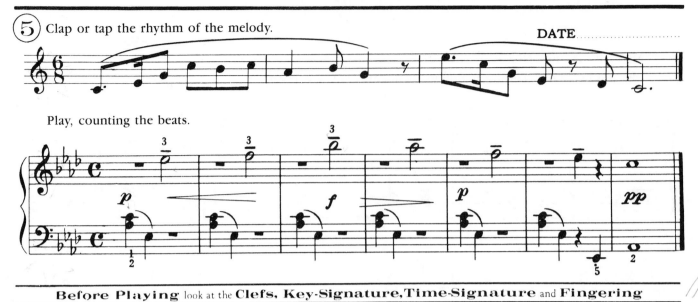

Play, counting the beats.

Before Playing look at the **Clefs, Key-Signature, Time-Signature** and **Fingering**

EAR TEST EXERCISES

1. Play the following. Listen to the last two chords of each phrase. Identify the cadences as perfect or authentic (V-I) or plagal (IV-I).

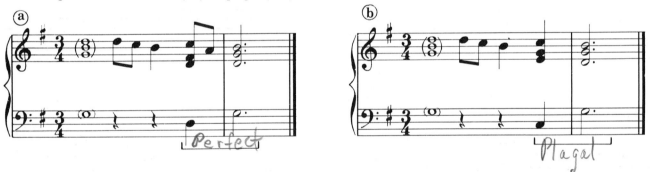

2. Look carefully at this tune. Name the key, then clap or tap the rhythm. Play the tune (a) looking at the music; (b) from memory.

3. Play, then hum the two notes of each interval. Name the interval.

4. Play, then identify each of the following:

PLAY ONE SET EVERY DAY

★ FOUR STAR TEST No. 1 ★
AT THE LESSON WITH THE TEACHER

1. Clap or tap the rhythm of the melody.

2. Answer these questions before playing the following pieces:
   What is the time signature?
   In what key is the piece written?
   What is the tempo?

3. Play these pieces while your teacher times the reading.

FOR EAR TESTS SEE PAGES 37, 38 and 39

F.H. 8531

DAILY SIGHT READING FOR TEST No. 2

①

This piece is in __3/4__ time. It is in the key of _D major_ and has __2__ sharps/flats.
Play, counting the beats.

TELEMANN

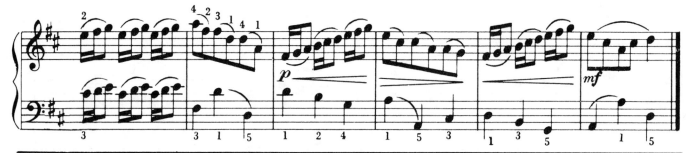

Before Playing look at the **Clefs, Key-Signature, Time-Signature** and **Fingering**

②

Put an X under each measure in which you find staccato notes, then play, naming the left-hand notes.
Play again, naming the right-hand notes.

KUHLAU

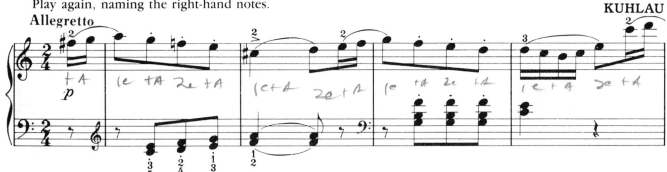

Clap or tap the rhythm of the melody.

F.H. 8531

PLAY ONE SET EVERY DAY

③ Mark all the dominant chords (V) with an X.
Play this piece while singing any voice (part).

Con moto

OLD ENGLISH TUNE

Before Playing look at the **Clefs, Key-Signature, Time-Signature** and **Fingering**

④

The tempo of this piece is _____Andante_____ , which means _____
Trace the slurs and phrase marks and copy all the expression marks.
Play with correct expression.

Andante

DUVERNOY

The expression marks found in this piece are: _____

PLAY ONE SET EVERY DAY

F.H. 8531

DAILY SIGHT READING FOR TEST No. 2

⑤ Clap or tap the rhythm of the melody.

DATE...........................

Before Playing look at the **Clefs, Key-Signature, Time-Signature** and **Fingering**

EAR TEST EXERCISES

1. Play the following. Listen to the last two chords of each phrase. Identify the cadences as perfect or authentic (V-I) or plagal (IV-I).

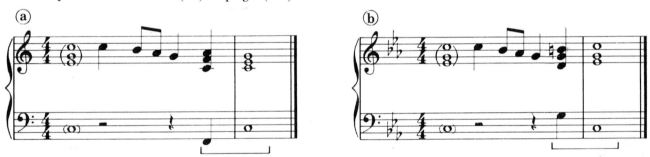

2. Look carefully at this tune. Name the key, then clap or tap the rhythm. Play the tune (a) looking at the music; (b) from memory.

3. Play, then hum the two notes of each interval. Name the interval.

4. Play, then identify each of the following:

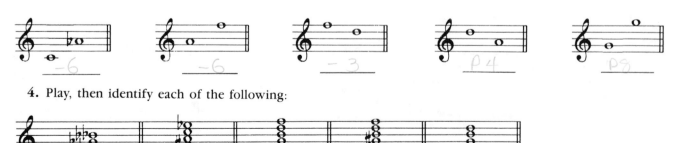

PLAY ONE SET EVERY DAY

★ FOUR STAR TEST No. 2 ★

AT THE LESSON WITH THE TEACHER

11

1. Clap or tap the rhythm of the melody.

2. Answer these questions before playing the following pieces:
What is the time signature?
In what key is the piece written?
What is the tempo?

3. Play these pieces while your teacher times the reading.

Larghetto espressivo

OLD ENGLISH TUNE

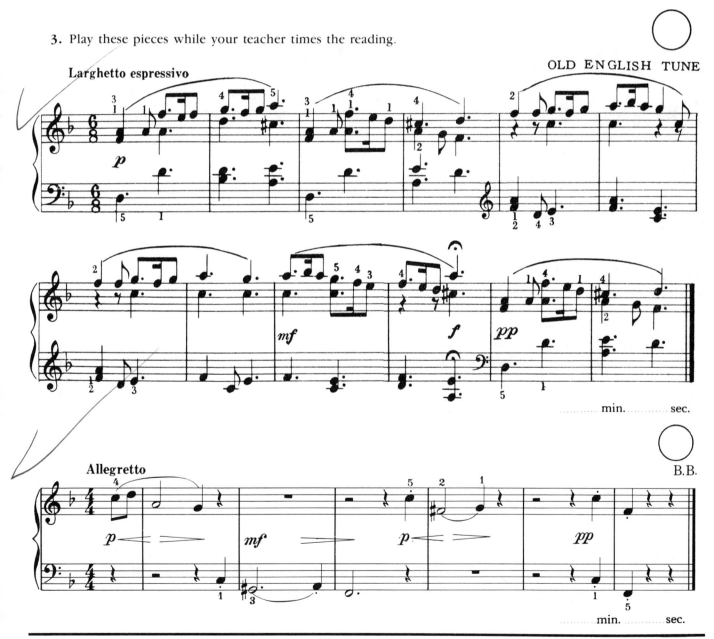

...........min...........sec.

Allegretto

B.B.

...........min...........sec.

F.H. 8531

FOR EAR TESTS SEE PAGES 37, 38 and 39

DAILY SIGHT READING FOR TEST No. 3

① DATE Nov 9th

This piece is in $\frac{4}{4}$ time. It is in the key of G + and has 1 sharps/flats.
Play, counting the beats.

BEETHOVEN

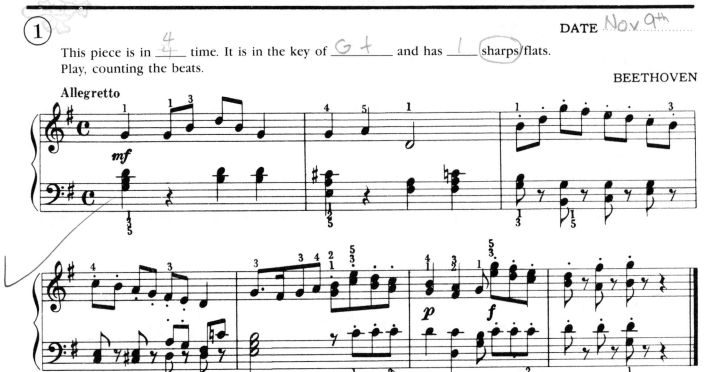

Before Playing look at the **Clefs, Key-Signature, Time-Signature** and **Fingering**

② DATE ....

Put an X under each broken triad, then play, naming the left-hand notes.
Play again, naming the right-hand notes.

HUMMEL

Clap or tap the rhythm of the melody.

F.H. 8531

PLAY ONE SET EVERY DAY

DAILY SIGHT READING FOR TEST No. 3

③

Mark all the tonic chords (I) with an X.
Play this hymn tune harmonization while singing any voice (part).

DATE

SPOHR

Before Playing look at the **Clefs, Key-Signature, Time-Signature** and **Fingering**

④

DATE

The tempo of this piece is _____ , which means _____
Trace the slurs and phrase marks and copy all the expression marks.
Play with correct expression.

Lento

VOGEL

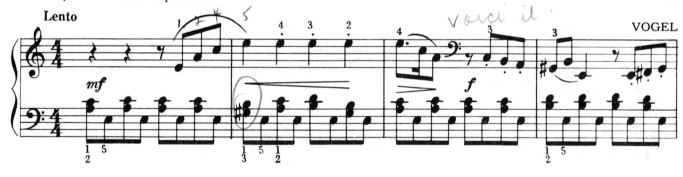

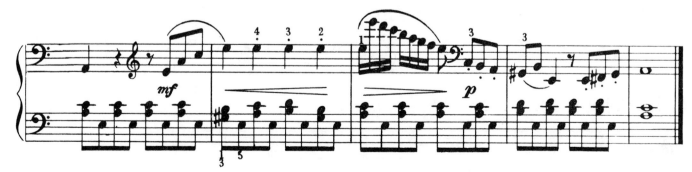

The expression marks found in this piece are: _____

F.H. 8531

PLAY ONE SET EVERY DAY

⑤ Clap or tap the rhythm of the melody.

Before Playing look at the **Clefs, Key-Signature, Time-Signature** and **Fingering**

EAR TEST EXERCISES

1. Play the following. Listen to the last two chords of each phrase. Identify the cadences as perfect or authentic (V-I) or plagal (IV-I).

ⓐ   ⓑ

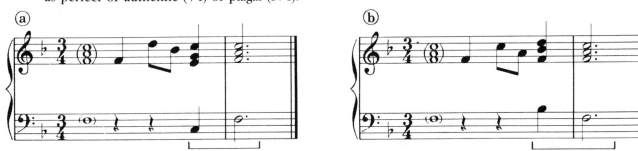

2. Look carefully at this tune. Name the key, then clap or tap the rhythm. Play the tune (a) looking at the music; (b) from memory.

3. Play, then hum the two notes of each interval. Name the interval.

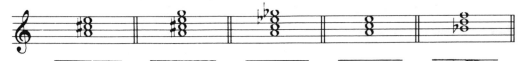

4. Play, then identify each of the following:

PLAY ONE SET EVERY DAY

★ FOUR STAR TEST No. 3 ★

AT THE LESSON WITH THE TEACHER

1. Clap or tap the rhythm of the melody.

2. Answer these questions before playing the following pieces:
What is the time signature?
In what key is the piece written?
What is the tempo?

3. Play these pieces while your teacher times the reading.

LISZT

.... min. .... sec.

PURCELL

.... min. .... sec.

FOR EAR TESTS SEE PAGES 37, 38 and 39

F.H. 8531

DAILY SIGHT READING FOR TEST No. 4

(1)

This piece is in $\frac{2}{2}$ time. It is in the key of e — and has 1 sharps/flats. Play, counting the beats.

Allegretto

KELLEGREW

Before Playing look at the **Clefs, Key-Signature, Time-Signature** and **Fingering**

(2)

DATE

Put an X under each appearance of the rhythmic pattern ♩ ♩ ♩ ♩ , then play, naming the left-hand notes. Play again, naming the right-hand notes.

Andante

HUMMEL

Clap or tap the rhythm of the melody.

PLAY ONE SET EVERY DAY

③   **DATE** ....

Mark all the dominant chords (V) with an X.

Play this old church melody harmonization while singing any voice (part).

Before Playing look at the **Clefs, Key-Signature, Time-Signature** and **Fingering**

④   **DATE** ....

The tempo of this piece is _____ , which means _____

Trace the slurs and phrase marks and copy all the expression marks.

Play with correct expression.

The expression marks found in this piece are: _____

PLAY ONE SET EVERY DAY

F.H. 8531

DATE ....

(5) Clap or tap the rhythm of the melody.

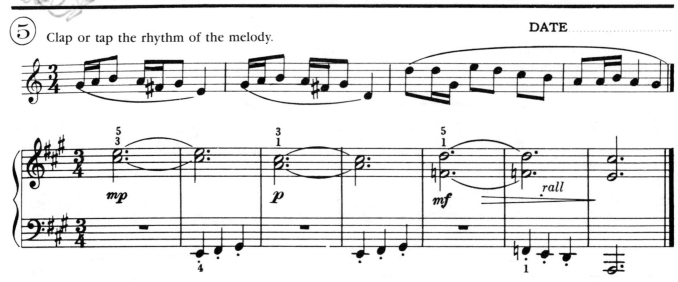

mp   *p*   *mf*   *rall*

Before Playing look at the **Clefs, Key-Signature, Time-Signature** and **Fingering**

Plagal drops a 4th or rises a 5th   IV   I
Perfect drops a 5th " " " 4th   V   I

Cadences

EAR TEST EXERCISES

1. Play the following. Listen to the last two chords of each phrase. Identify the cadences as perfect or authentic (V-I) or Plagal (IV-I).

   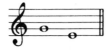

(a)   (b)

2. Look carefully at this tune. Name the key, then clap or tap the rhythm. Play the tune
   (a) looking at the music; (b) from memory.

3. Play, then hum the two notes of each interval. Name the interval.

___   ___   ___   ___   ___

4. Play, then identify each of the following:

___   ___   ___   ___   ___

19

★ FOUR STAR TEST No. 4 ★

AT THE LESSON WITH THE TEACHER

1. Clap or tap the rhythm of the melody.

2. Answer these questions before playing the following pieces:
What is the time signature?
In what key is the piece written?
What is the tempo?

3. Play these pieces while your teacher times the reading.

SCHUBERT

.... min .... sec.

B.B.

.... min .... sec.

FOR EAR TESTS SEE PAGES 37, 38 and 39

F.H. 8531

DAILY SIGHT READING <small>FOR TEST</small> No. 5

(1)

This piece is in _____ time. It is in the key of _____ and has _____ sharps/flats.
Play, counting the beats.

Before Playing look at the **Clefs, Key-Signature, Time-Signature** and **Fingering**

(2)

Put an X under each appearance of the rhythmic pattern ♩. ♪ ♩ , then play, naming the left-hand notes.
Play again, naming the right-hand notes.

Clap or tap the rhythm of the melody.

F.H. 8531 | **PLAY ONE SET EVERY DAY**

DAILY SIGHT READING <small>FOR TEST</small> No. 5

③

Mark all the subdominant chords (IV) with an X.
Play this piece while singing any voice (part).

DATE

GLUCK

Allegretto

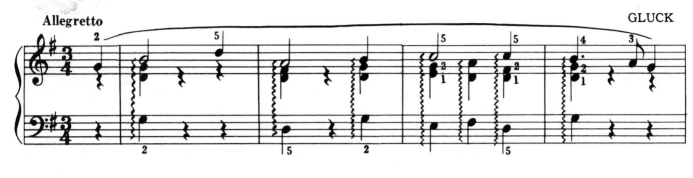

Before Playing look at the **Clefs, Key-Signature, Time-Signature** and **Fingering**

④

The tempo of this piece is _____ , which means _____
Trace the slurs and phrase marks and copy all the expression marks.
Play with correct expression.

DATE

ANDRÉ

Allegretto

The expression marks found in this piece are: _____

PLAY ONE SET EVERY DAY

F.H. 8531

5 Clap or tap the rhythm of the melody.   DATE ....

Before Playing look at the **Clefs, Key-Signature, Time-Signature** and **Fingering**

EAR TEST EXERCISES

1. Play the following. Listen to the last two chords of each phrase. Identify the cadences as perfect or authentic (V-I) or Plagal (IV-I).

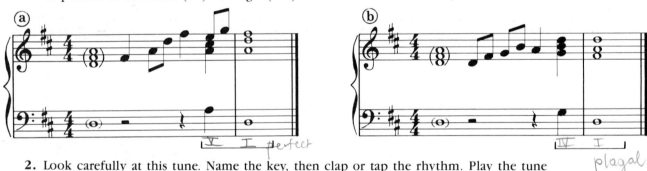

V I perfect   IV I plagal

2. Look carefully at this tune. Name the key, then clap or tap the rhythm. Play the tune (a) looking at the music; (b) from memory.

3. Play, then hum the two notes of each interval. Name the interval.

P 5   P 4   −6   +2   +6

4. Play, then identify each of the following:

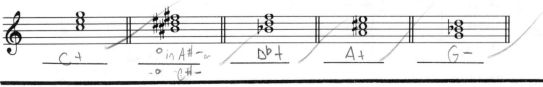

C +   ° in A# or   Db +   A +   G −
        ° C#

★ FOUR STAR TEST No. 5 ★

AT THE LESSON WITH THE TEACHER

1. Clap or tap the rhythm of the melody.

2. Answer these questions before playing the following pieces:
What is the time signature?
In what key is the piece written?
What is the tempo?

3. Play these pieces while your teacher times the reading.

OLD FOLK SONG

.... min. .... sec.

A SLOW WALTZ gr. 5

Tempo di Valse

KABALEVSKY

.... min. .... sec.

FOR EAR TESTS SEE PAGES 37, 38 and 39

F.H. 8531

DAILY SIGHT READING <small>FOR TEST</small> No. 6

①

DATE *Sept 16th/1994*

This piece is in __3/4__ time. It is in the key of __G+__ and has __1__ sharps/~~flats~~.
Play, counting the beats.

TELEMANN

Before Playing look at the **Clefs, Key-Signature, Time-Signature** and **Fingering**

②

DATE ....

Put an X under each sharp sign and natural sign, then play, naming the left-hand notes.
Play again, naming the right-hand notes.

HUMMEL

Clap or tap the rhythm of the melody.

PLAY ONE SET EVERY DAY

DAILY SIGHT READING FOR TEST No. 6

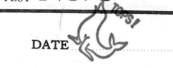

③ Mark all the tonic chords (I) with an X.
Play this hymn tune harmonization while singing any voice (part).

HAYDN

Before Playing look at the **Clefs, Key-Signature, Time-Signature** and **Fingering**

④   DATE.........................

The tempo of this piece is _____ , which means _____ .
Trace the slurs and phrase marks and copy all the expression marks.
Play with correct expression.

Tempo di Valse   B. B.

The expression marks found in this piece are: _____

PLAY ONE SET EVERY DAY   F.H. 8531

DAILY SIGHT READING ^{FOR TEST} No. 6

⑤ Clap or tap the rhythm of the melody.   DATE ....

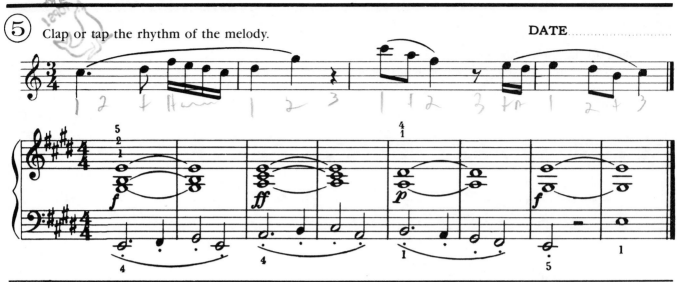

Before Playing look at the **Clefs, Key-Signature, Time-Signature** and **Fingering**

EAR TEST EXERCISES

1. Play the following. Listen to the last two chords of each phrase. Identify the cadences as perfect or authentic (V-I) or plagal (IV-I).

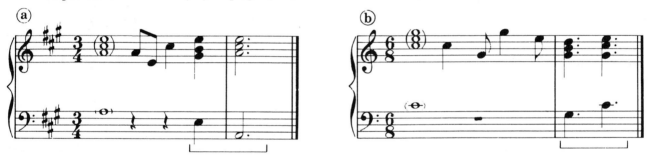

2. Look carefully at this tune. Name the key, then clap or tap the rhythm. Play the tune (a) looking at the music; (b) from memory.

3. Play, then hum the two notes of each interval. Name the interval.

4. Play, then identify each of the following:

F.H. 8531   **PLAY ONE SET EVERY DAY**

1. Clap or tap the rhythm of the melody.

2. Answer these questions before playing the following pieces:
What is the time signature?
In what key is the piece written?
What is the tempo?

3. Play these pieces while your teacher times the reading.

Tempo di Valse

VOGEL

.... min. .... sec.

Allegro

E.C.M.

.... min. .... sec.

FOR EAR TESTS SEE PAGES 37, 38 and 39

F.H. 8531

28

DAILY SIGHT READING ^{FOR TEST} No. 7

① DATE

This piece is in _____ time. It is in the key of _____ and has _____ sharps/flats.
Play, counting the beats.

Before Playing look at the **Clefs, Key-Signature, Time-Signature** and **Fingering**

② DATE

Put an X under each appearance of the rhythmic pattern ♩♪♪♩, then play, naming the left-hand notes.
Play again, naming the right-hand notes.

Clap or tap the rhythm of the melody.

F.H. 8531

PLAY ONE SET EVERY DAY

③

Mark all the tonic chords (I) with an X.
Play this piece while singing the melody.

Tempo di mazurka

REBIKOV

Before Playing look at the **Clefs, Key-Signature, Time-Signature** and **Fingering**

④

The tempo of this piece is _____ , which means _____
Trace the slurs and phrase marks and copy all the expression marks.
Play with correct expression.

Andante

MOZART

The expression marks found in this piece are: _____

⑤ Clap or tap the rhythm of the melody.

DATE....................

Before Playing look at the **Clefs, Key-Signature, Time-Signature** and **Fingering**

EAR TEST EXERCISES

1. Play the following. Listen to the last two chords of each phrase. Identify the cadences
as perfect or authentic (V-I) or plagal (IV-I).

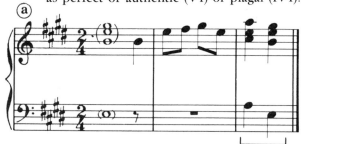

2. Look carefully at this tune. Name the key, then clap or tap the rhythm. Play the tune
(a) looking at the music; (b) from memory.

3. Play, then hum the two notes of each interval. Name the interval.

  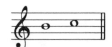 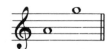 

4. Play, then identify each of the following:

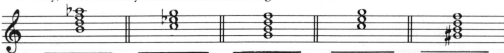

PLAY ONE SET EVERY DAY

1. Clap or tap the rhythm of the melody.

2. Answer these questions before playing the following pieces:
   What is the time signature?
   In what key is the piece written?
   What is the tempo?

3. Play these pieces while your teacher times the reading.

Allegro   HÄSSLER

.... min. .... sec.

EIGES

Allegretto

.... min. .... sec.

F.H. 8531

FOR EAR TESTS SEE PAGES 37, 38 and 39

DAILY SIGHT READING <small>FOR TEST</small> No. 8

①   DATE ....

This piece is in _____ time. It is in the key of _____ and has _____ sharps/flats.
Play, counting the beats.

ZIPOLI

Before Playing look at the **Clefs, Key-Signature, Time-Signature** and **Fingering**

---

②   DATE ....

Put an X under each sharp sign and natural sign, then play, naming the left-hand notes.
Play again, naming the right-hand notes.

MOZART

Clap or tap the rhythm of the melody.

PLAY ONE SET EVERY DAY

③

Mark all the broken tonic chords (I) with an X.
Play this piece while singing the top voice (part).

Grazioso

PURCELL

Before Playing look at the **Clefs, Key-Signature, Time-Signature** and **Fingering**

④

The tempo of this piece is _____ , which means _____
Trace the slurs and phrase marks and copy all the expression marks.
Play with correct expression.

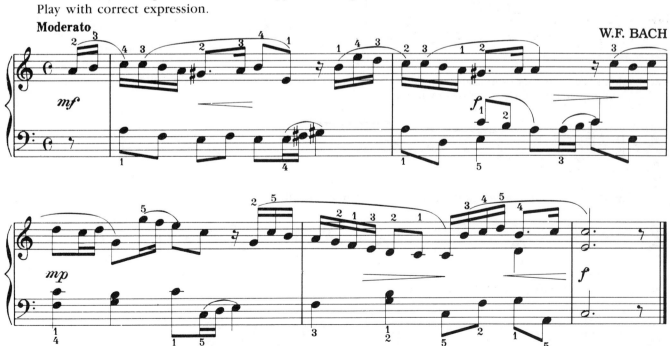

Moderato

W.F. BACH

The expression marks found in this piece are: _____

PLAY ONE SET EVERY DAY

F.H. 8531

⑤ Clap or tap the rhythm of the melody.

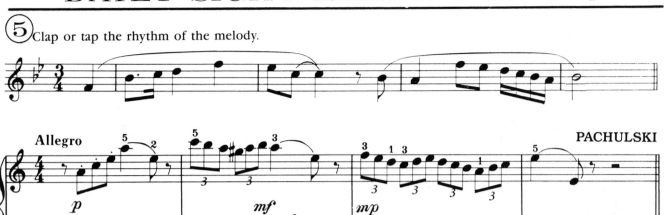

Allegro   PACHULSKI

Before Playing look at the **Clefs, Key-Signature, Time-Signature** and **Fingering**

EAR TEST EXERCISES

1. Play the following. Listen to the last two chords of each phrase. Identify the cadences as perfect or authentic (V-I) or plagal (IV-I).

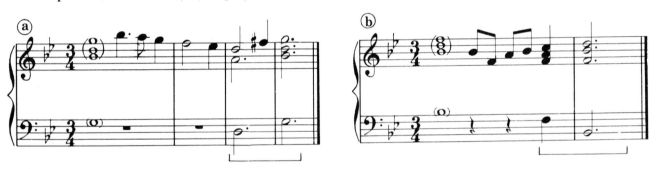

2. Look carefully at this tune. Name the key, then clap or tap the rhythm. Play the tune (a) looking at the music; (b) from memory.

3. Play, then hum the two notes of each interval. Name the interval.

_____   _____   _____   _____   _____

4. Play, then identify each of the following:

_____   _____   _____   _____   _____

PLAY ONE SET EVERY DAY

★ FOUR STAR TEST No. 8 ★

AT THE LESSON WITH THE TEACHER

1. Clap or tap the rhythm of the melody. ◯

2. Answer these questions before playing the following piece: ◯
What is the time signature?
In what key is the piece written?
What is the tempo?

3. Play this piece while your teacher times the reading. ◯

Moderato   GRÜNEWALD

min. .... sec.

4. Clap or tap the rhythm of the melody. ◯

FOR EAR TESTS SEE PAGES 37, 38 and 39

F.H. 8531

★ FINAL TEST ★

This Test must be given before filling in and signing the Certificate of Merit.

AT THE LESSON WITH THE TEACHER

1. The teacher plays the tonic chord, then plays a short phrase in a major or minor key twice. The phrase will end with a perfect or plagal cadence, as in the examples shown below. (The student must not see the keyboard or look at the music.)

   The student then identifies the cadence by name or by symbols.

2. The teacher names the key, plays the tonic triad, then plays a melody of approximately 9 notes twice. (The student must not see the keyboard or look at the music.)

The student must play back the same melody from memory (by ear).

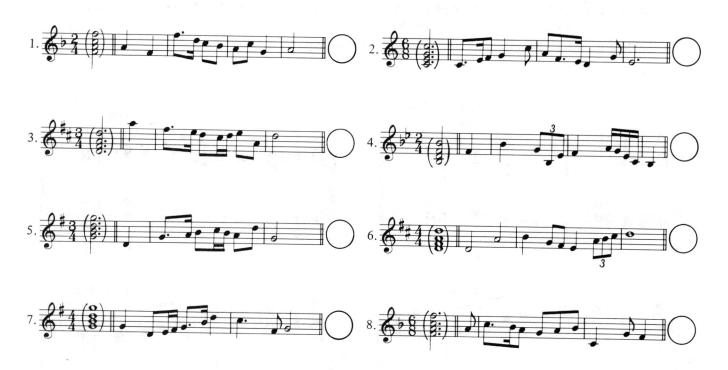

3. The teacher plays the first note of any of the intervals shown below and the student then sings or hums the other note; OR

The teacher plays the interval in broken form, and the student identifies the interval by ear. (The student must not see the keyboard or look at the music.)

The intervals may be played in whichever octave is best suited to the range of the student's voice.

Major seconds (above a given note):

Minor seconds (above a given note):

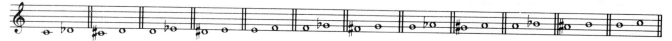

Major thirds (above a given note):

Minor thirds (above a given note):

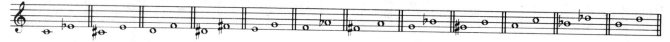

Perfect fourths (above a given note):

Perfect fifths (above a given note):

Major sixths (above a given note):

Minor sixths (above a given note):

Minor sevenths (above a given note):

Perfect octaves (above a given note):

Major seconds (below a given note):

Minor sixths (below a given note):

Major thirds (below a given note):

Minor thirds (below a given note):

Perfect fourths (below a given note):

Perfect fifths (below a given note):

Major sevenths (below a given note):

Perfect octaves (below a given note):

4. The teacher plays a root position major or minor triad or dominant or diminished seventh chord once only, in solid form and close position. The student must identify the chord without looking at the keyboard.

Major Triads:

Minor Triads:

Dominant seventh chords:

Diminished Seventh chords:

Certificate of Merit

This certifies that

----

has completed

FOUR STAR SIGHT READING

Level 8

Teacher . . . .

Date . . . .